MW01602083

EXPLORING RECYCLING AND TRASH SEGREGATION

Coloring book

Rosa Moss

Table of Content

Different Bins

Glass materials, like glass bottles, jars, and jugs, should go in the glass bin.

Organic materials, like food scraps and garden waste, belong in the organic bin.

Plastic materials, such as plastic bottles and shampoo containers, go into the plastic bin.

Paper materials, such as milk cartons, orange cartons, and cereal boxes, find their place in the paper bin.

1

Bin with Organic Materials

Brown

Bin with Glass Materials

Green

Bin with Plastic Materials

Orange

Blue

Bin with Paper Materials

2

Why Separate?

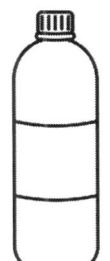

By sorting your waste into the right bins, you help recycling centers process the materials more efficiently.

This reduces the amount of waste that ends up in landfills and helps protect our environment.

Organic waste is biodegradable, which means it can decompose naturally and enrich the soil.

When you throw organic waste into the right bin, it gets turned into compost.

Compost is like a superfood for plants, helping them grow strong and healthy.

4

Banana peel

Fish Bones

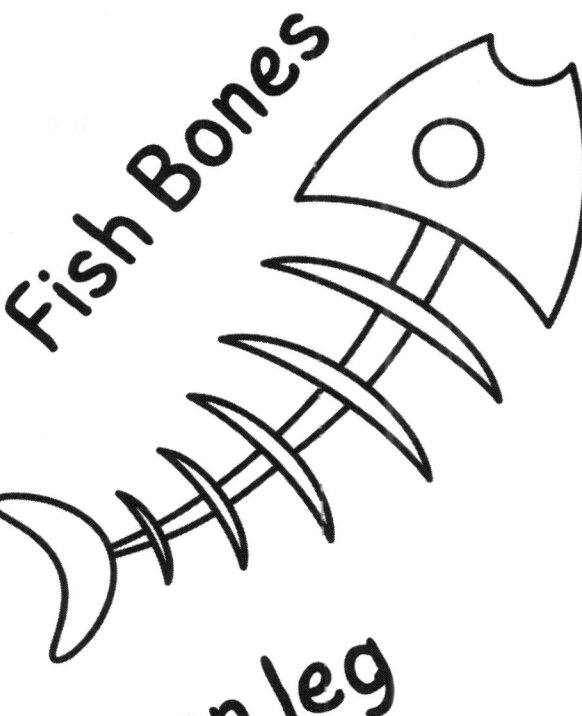

Apple core

Chicken leg

Orange peel

Eggshell

Glass is a valuable material that can be recycled over and over again.

Items like glass bottles, jars, and jugs can be transformed into new glass products.

Recycling glass saves energy and raw materials, reducing the environmental impact.

Glass Bottle

Glass

Jar

Jug

7

Plastic Recycling

Plastic materials, like plastic bottles and shampoo containers, can be recycled to create new plastic products.

Proper disposal and recycling of plastics help prevent pollution, especially in oceans where plastic waste harms marine life.

Shampoo Container

Plastic Bottle

Laundry Detergent
Bottle

9

Paper Recycling

Milk cartons, orange cartons, and cereal boxes are made of paper materials that can be recycled.

Recycling paper helps save trees and reduces deforestation, which is vital for a healthy environment.

Orange Carton

Milk Carton

Cereal Box

11

Metal Recycling

Items like soda cans and tin cans can be recycled to create new metal products.

Recycling metals conserves valuable resources, reduces the need for mining, and lowers energy consumption.

Soda Can

Tin Can

Garbage / Recycling trucks are big, strong vehicles that pick up and take away our trash to keep our neighborhoods clean.

They make sure our waste is properly collected and taken to the right place for disposal or recycling.

Recycling Truck

Trash collectors keep our streets clear of garbage.

Show appreciation for the people who collect and dispose of waste in our communities.

Let's give them a big thank you for all they do to keep the globe clean.

TRASH
COLLECTOR

17

Your step into recycling

Ask your parents to consider creating separate spaces at home for different types of waste: recycling bins, garbage cans, and compost bins.

Label these zones so everyone in the family knows where each type of waste belongs

18

Garbage Can

Compost Bin

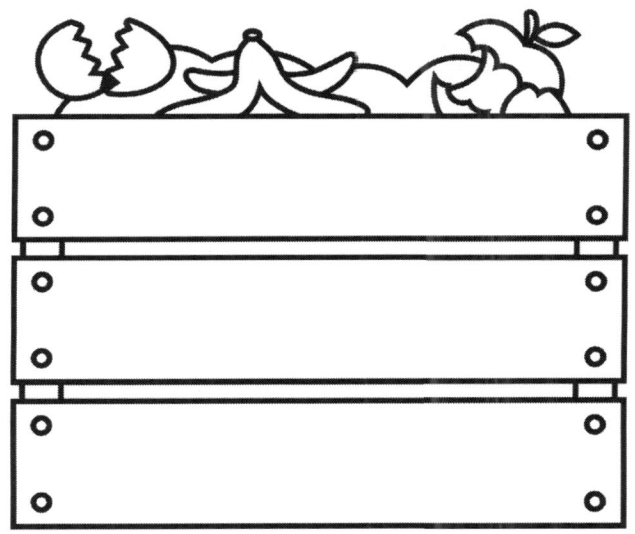

Recycling Bin

19

Garbage bags should be used for waste that can't be recycled or composted.

Be sure to tie the bag securely before placing it in the garbage can.

Recycling bins are for items that can be recycled.

Recycling boxes are handy for collecting items like newspapers, magazines, and cardboard.

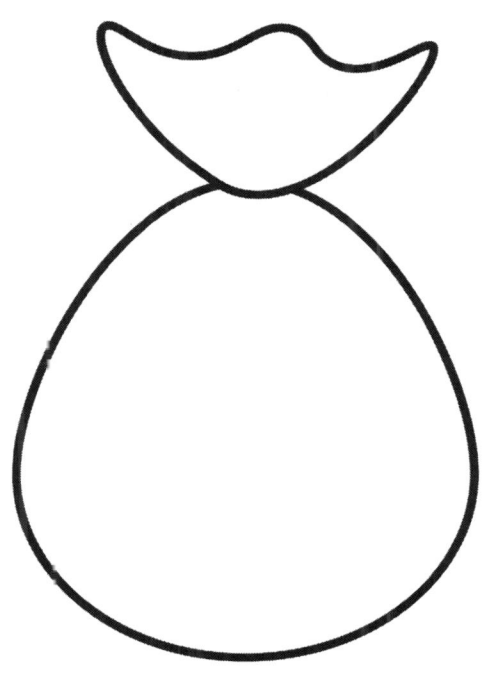

Garbage Bag

Box

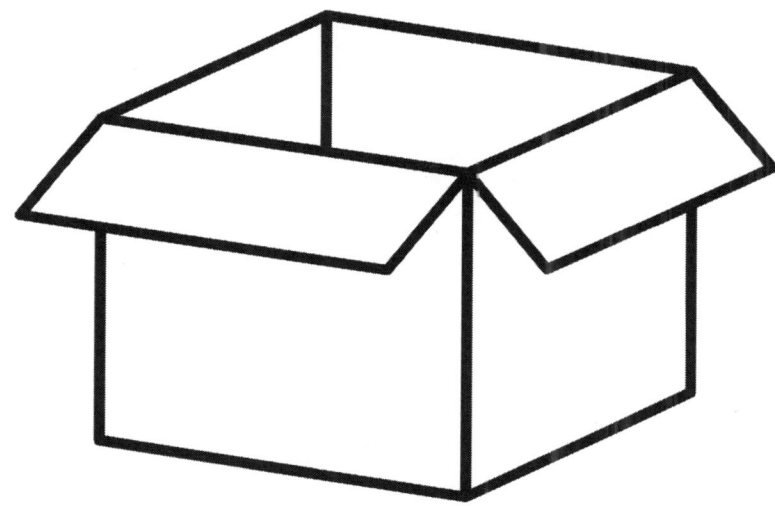

Recycling Bin

21

You can play a significant role in taking care of our beautiful Earth.

Think of our planet as your home, your playground, your everything. It's a place we all share, and it's our responsibility to care for it.

Recycling is one of the simplest and the most powerful ways to do that.

Made in the USA
Las Vegas, NV
02 April 2025

20426161R00017